P9-CBT-542

DESIGN IT!

FAIRY GARDEN DESIGN

Alix Wood

Gareth Stevens
PUBLISHING

Please visit our website, **www.garethstevens.com**.
For a free color catalog of all our high-quality books,
call toll free 1-800-542-2595 or fax 1-877-542-2596

Cataloging-in-Publication Data
Names: Wood, Alix.
Title: Fairy garden design / Alix Wood.
Description: New York : Gareth Stevens Publishing, 2018. | Series: Design it! | Includes index.
Identifiers: ISBN 9781538208021 (pbk.) | ISBN 9781538207925 (library bound) |
ISBN 9781538207802 (6 pack)
Subjects: LCSH: Gardens, Miniature--Juvenile literature. | Gardening for children--Juvenile literature. |
Fairies in art--Juvenile literature. | Miniature decorative design.
Classification: LCC SB433.5 W66 2018 | DDC 635.083--dc23

First Edition

Published in 2018 by
Gareth Stevens Publishing
111 East 14th Street, Suite 349
New York, NY 10003

Copyright © 2018 Alix Wood Books

Produced for Gareth Stevens by Alix Wood Books
Designed by Alix Wood
Editor: Eloise Macgregor
Projects created by Deborah Robbins
Editor for Gareth Stevens: Kerri O'Donnell

Photo credits: Cover, 1, 3, 4 bottom, 5 top, 6 bottom, 7 top left and right, 8, 9, 10, 11 top and middle, 12, 13, 16 right, 17 top, 18, 19 top, 20, 21 top left and right, 22, 23 top and bottom, 24, 25, 26, 27 © Chris Robbins Photography; 4 top © Adobe Stock Images; 5 bottom, 7 bottom left and right, 11 bottom, 14, 15, 16 left, 17 middle and bottom, 19 bottom, 21 bottom, 23 middle, 28, 29 © Alix Wood; 6 top © Shutterstock; 19 middle © Jessie Lynn McMains

All rights reserved. No part of this book may be reproduced in any form
without permission from the publisher, except by reviewer.

Printed in the United States of America
CPSIA compliance information: Batch #CS17GS: For further information contact Gareth Stevens, New York, New York at 1-800-542-2595.

CONTENTS

FAIRY GARDENING

Fairies are tiny people thought to have **magical** powers. Not everyone believes fairies are real. Why not create a fairy garden and see if any come? These cute gardens are fun to design. If you don't have a yard that's no problem. You can design them to go indoors, too.

CHOOSING A CONTAINER

Just about any container is suitable for a fairy garden. You could use an old pail or even a tire. This garden was created inside an old broken refrigerator drawer! To help your plants thrive, make sure there are **drainage** holes in your container.

A fairy garden is a tiny version of a real garden. Just like with a doll's house, the garden will look best if the **scale** is the same. The scale is how much smaller everything is than it is in real life.

Design Tips

A popular scale for fairy gardens is 1:12. Anything that is 1 foot (30 cm) tall in real life would be scaled down to 1 inch (2.5 cm) tall for the fairy garden.

This tepee is just like the full-size one to its right, but it is 1:12 scale.

You could sketch a garden plan first to check if everything works. You don't have to though. You can just get creating, and add things or take things away if they don't look good.

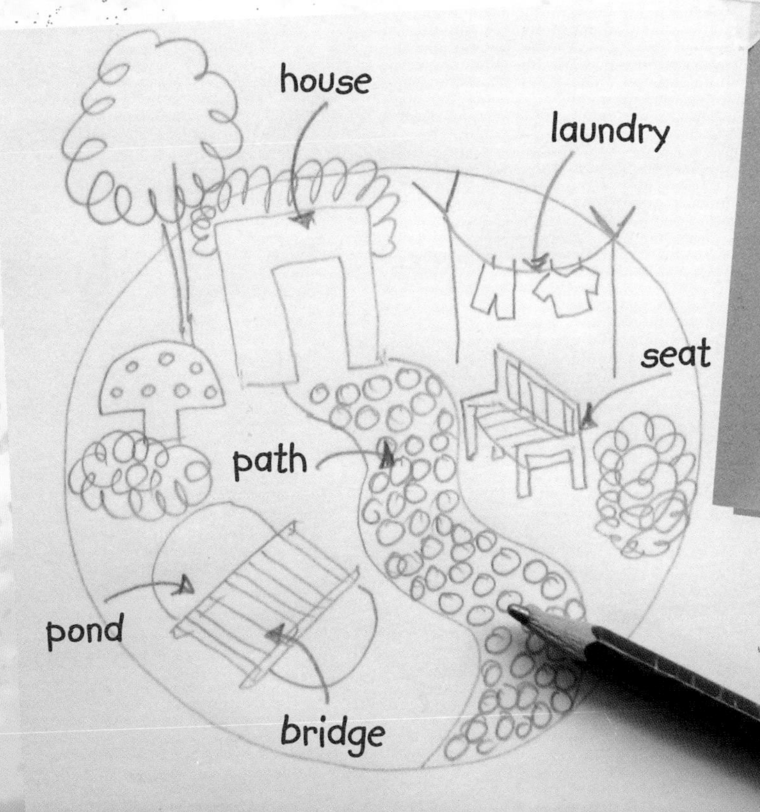

GETTING STARTED

You can make everything for your fairy garden using everyday objects. Start collecting. You'll find you start looking at everything and imagining how you could use them in your fairy garden! Get **inventive** — a shell could make a fairy bathtub, an acorn top could be a plate or a hat. Once you get the bug you'll be able to think up lots of your own ideas.

USEFUL THINGS

bottle tops - for paths or seats

necklaces - use for fencing, as a tree garland, or as chain for a swing

wire - twist to make furniture

gravel - good for patios and paths

corks - can be pushed into the soil to make pathways

pinecones - break into pieces to use as roof shingles

small pots and thimbles - use as garden decorations

twigs - useful for furniture, trees, etc.

When you choose plants for your fairy garden, you will want their scale to look right. Try to find plants with small leaves. You can trim the bottom leaves off a small shrub to make it look like a tree. Moss makes great grass. Place the container where the plants will get the **conditions** they need, either sunny or shady depending on the plants you choose.

This shrub was created by cutting the ends off pampas grass, tying them with rubber bands and pushing them into the soil.

TURN A CUTTING INTO A TREE

1. This heather plant has nice, small leaves and a tree-like stalk. It will make quite a **convincing** tree.

2. Cut the lower branches off to create a tree trunk. Trim the top into a tree-like shape.

FAIRY HOUSES

One of the first projects you might like to make for your fairy garden is a fairy house. Visiting fairies will want somewhere to keep out of the weather or to call home.

YOU WILL NEED:

- a yogurt cup
- scissors
- some twigs
- rubber bands
- strong glue
- masking tape
- some moss and ivy
- tiny craft flowers

1

Find your yogurt cup. Using scissors, cut an opening into it, like the one pictured above. This will be your doorway. Cover the cup in masking tape.

2

Cut the twigs to the same length as the yogurt cup. You may need an adult to help you. Squeeze some glue onto the cup. Stick your twigs into the glue. Hold the twigs in place with the rubber bands.

Design Tips

You can use **double-sided tape** to stick your twigs in place, instead. Peel off the second protective layer from the tape once you have covered your cup. One by one, place the twigs along the tape.

3

Cut shorter lengths of twig to fit above the doorway. Hold all the twigs in place with the rubber bands until the glue dries.

4

You could decorate your fairy house with flowers. You can use icing flowers like these, or make some out of colored card stock. You will need to protect the flowers from damp weather.

Arrange some moss and ivy over the roof of your fairy house.

TOADSTOOLS

You can make these model toadstools from salt dough or modeling clay. It is important to **varnish** the models if they are to be kept for any length of time. Otherwise, the moist soil will ruin them. Modeling clay will usually last longest.

YOU WILL NEED:

- clay or salt dough
- two paintbrushes
- acrylic paint
- strong glue
- a wooden stick or similar
- waterproof varnish
- a small cup or thimble

SALT DOUGH RECIPE

1 cup salt
2 cups flour
3/4 cup water
Mix the salt and flour together. Gradually stir in the water until it forms a dough. Knead the dough until smooth.

The models can be cooked in a medium oven or air dried. Once dry, seal the models with varnish to keep them from getting soggy. Ask an adult to help when you use the oven or the varnish.

1

Roll out the dough or clay to around 1/2 inch (1.3 cm) thick. Cut out some circles using a small cup or thimble. Scrunch up half the circles to make the bases of the toadstools.

2

Using a wooden stick or blunt knife, mark the underside of the toadstool caps. Then gently shape the caps by pressing your thumb into the center.

3

Leave the toadstool pieces to dry. When they are completely dry, stick each base to its cap using strong glue.

4

Paint the toadstools using acrylic paint. Make sure the red paint is dry before you put on the white spots or they will run.

Design Tips

If you want your toadstools to last, cover them all over in a coat of varnish. You may want an adult to help you as varnish can be messy and doesn't come off if you spill it on things. Wear old clothes and use an old paintbrush.

PARTY PENNANTS

Colorful pennants always give a garden a party atmosphere. These cute little pennants are sure to attract any passing fairies!

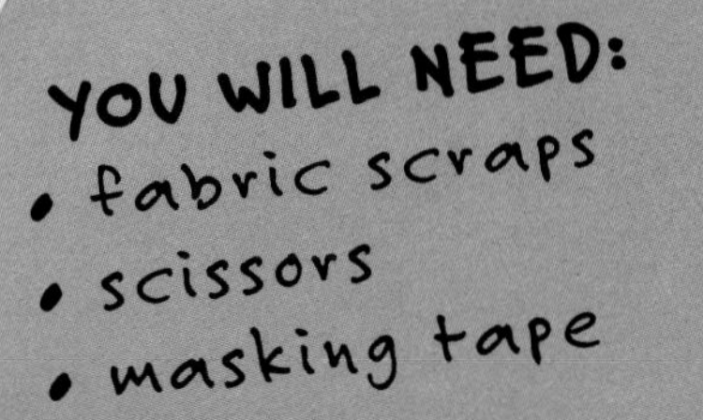

1

Place some masking tape along your strips of fabric. This keeps the fabric from fraying when you cut out your tiny triangles.

2

Using a pen, draw your triangles onto the masking tape. Try to keep them all the same size. You can use a ruler if you want.

3

Carefully cut out your fabric triangles. It is easiest to cut inwards on both sides, rather than turn the fabric. You may want an adult to help you.

4

Cut a length of masking tape and lay it sticky-side up. Carefully place your triangles along the tape, pattern-side up.

5

Lay a length of string along the tape. Fold the tape over to enclose the string. Trim the tape if necessary.

Tie the pennant's string to two twigs and push them into the soil in your garden.

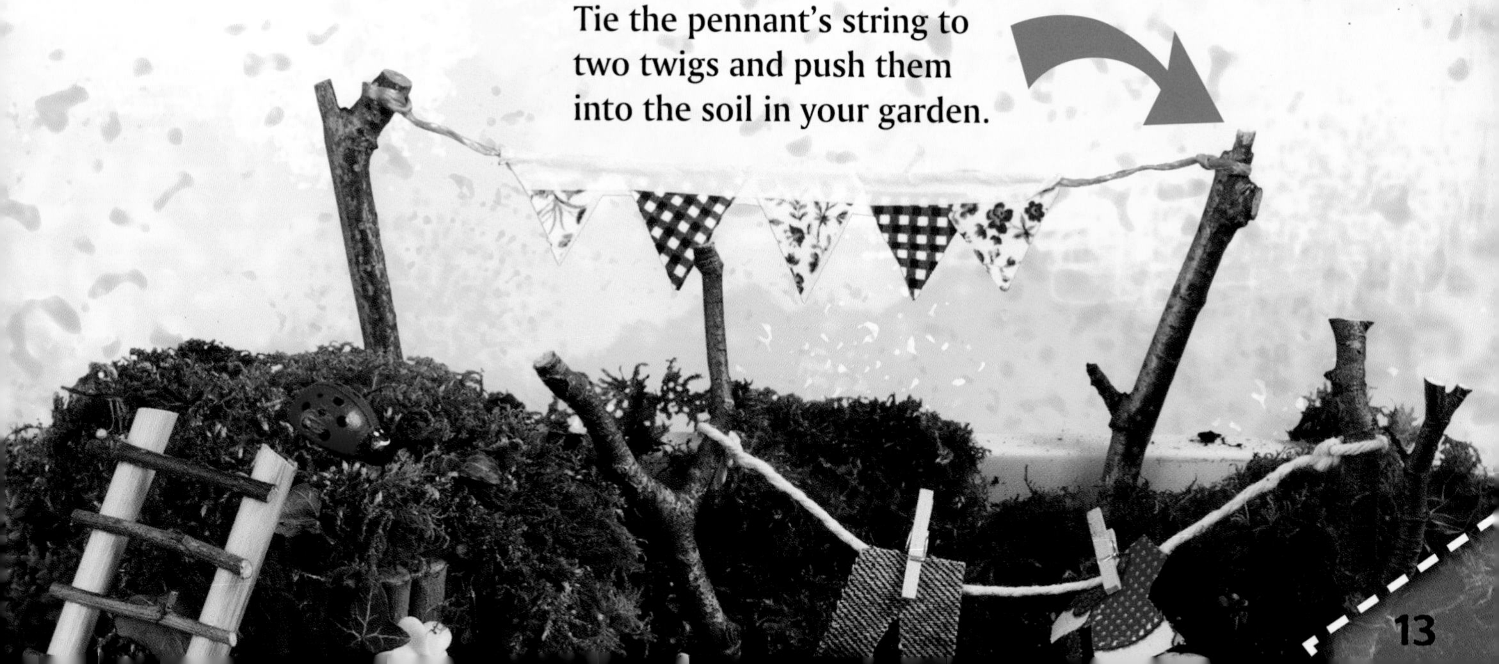

A FAIRY DOOR

Do you have a little hole in a tree or tree stump in your yard? Maybe the hole is being used as a shelter by fairies. Help them keep out the weather by making a cute fairy door.

Design Tips

You can decorate your fairy door in so many ways. Try gluing on buttons or beads to decorate your door. You could draw hinges using black marker. An acorn cap makes a cute doorknob.

YOU WILL NEED:

- craft sticks
- strong scissors
- some sequins
- a push pin
- some modeling clay

1

Choose six craft sticks to make into your door. These sticks were already painted. Plain wood sticks look good, too, though.

2

Cut one craft stick in half using strong scissors. You may need an adult to help you.

3

Glue the half craft sticks on the back of the fairy door. Place one near the top and one near the bottom. Leave until the glue dries. You could place something like a heavy book on the sticks to help press them down.

4

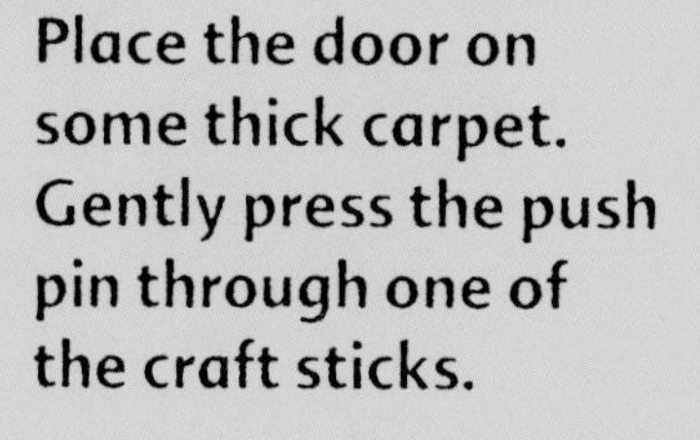

Place the door on some thick carpet. Gently press the push pin through one of the craft sticks.

5

If your push pin sticks through the back of the door, cover the point with modeling clay.

Now have fun decorating your fairy door. You could glue on some sequins.

FAIRY SWINGS

Fairies probably want to have fun while they are playing in their gardens. Try making these cute swings for your fairies to play on.

If you don't have a tire, you could always just make knots in your braided rope for the fairies to grip and swing on!

YOU WILL NEED:

- some string
- a small branch
- a toy tire

1

Take three pieces of string and tie them together at one end. Braid the string to make your rope. Thread a toy tire through the rope and tie it to a branch.

YOU WILL NEED:
- a cheap bracelet
- a craft stick
- scissors
- two twist ties

1

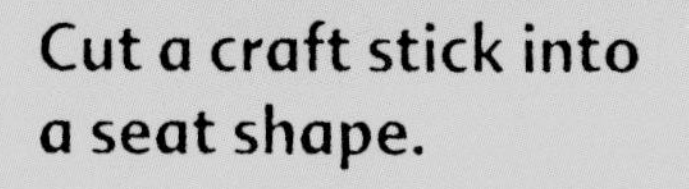

Cut a craft stick into a seat shape.

2

Peel the cover from two twist ties. Wrap the twist tie wire around either end of the swing seat.

3

Thread the wire through the ends of the bracelet. Attach your chain to a branch. You can use some more twist tie wire to do this.

MAKING PATHWAYS

Tiny pathways really add a sense of scale to your fairy garden. They help lead the eye to a **focal point**, too. Try making a winding path of stepping stones or a straight path bordered by twigs.

YOU WILL NEED:
- sticks
- stones or slate
- some **pea gravel**
- broken flowerpots
- corks

1

You can push corks into the soil to make a **realistic** stepping stone pathway.

2

Small pieces of slate or flat pebbles make a great path. You could add a stick border and then fill the gaps with pea gravel.

3

Pea gravel is very fine gravel. It makes great fairy paths and patios, because the small size helps match the fairy garden's tiny scale.

4

You can make a path or patio out of broken pots or tiles. Be careful of any sharp edges. To break up a flowerpot, first place it in a bag. This keeps the broken pieces from flying around and hurting you.

Fairies Welcome!

Design Tips

You could make a tiny "Welcome" sign out of craft sticks and glue. Put it at the end of your path to let the fairies know they are expected!

A RAMP OR BRIDGE

Try making this little wooden ramp for your garden. You can use it in a number of ways. It could be a ramp up into a fairy house, or you could use it as a bridge over a little pond.

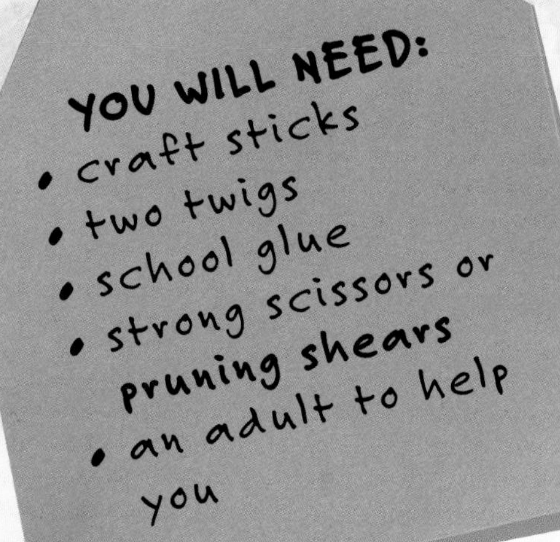

Some craft sticks and twigs can be tough to cut. It is best to ask an adult to help you.

1

Cut two twigs to the same length. These will form the supports for your ramp. Cut the craft sticks into equal smaller lengths. These will become the floorboards for your ramp.

2

Stick the craft stick floorboards to the twigs using school glue. It may help to press the twigs to a surface using modeling clay to keep them steady.

3

Continue to glue all of the floorboards to the twig supports. Leave the ramp to dry.

MAKE A FAIRY POND

YOU WILL NEED:

- a jar lid
- blue and orange acrylic paint
- school glue
- a paintbrush
- small stones

Paint the inside of a jar lid with school glue. Let it dry. Paint over the glue using blue acrylic paint. Once that is dry you could paint some orange goldfish in your pond. Coat the fish in school glue, too, once they are dry.

When all the paint and glue has dried, place the lid in your garden and surround it with stones. Fill your pond with water.

FAIRY LAUNDRY DAY

Even fairies have to have a wash day. Try making this cute clothesline filled with tiny fairy clothes. You could even make a laundry basket out of half a walnut shell or a bottle lid! You can buy the tiny clothespins from most craft stores.

YOU WILL NEED:

- clothespins
- fabric scraps
- string
- two twigs
- a pen
- scissors

Design Tips

You can make your own clothespins. Break off a tiny twig. Split it in half lengthwise, about halfway up the twig. Push the open end over the clothes to secure them to the clothesline.

1

Draw some tiny clothes on your fabric using a pen. Simple shapes work best as complicated ones can be hard to cut out.

2

Cut out your fairy clothes using scissors.

Cut or break the two twigs so they are a similar size. Y-shaped twigs are ideal, if you can find any. Tie a length of string between the two twigs.

Now it's time to pin your laundry on the clothesline. Decide where you want the clothesline to go, and push the twigs into the soil.

FAIRY LADDER

Fairies may need help to climb up into your flowerpot. Why not make them a fairy ladder!

YOU WILL NEED:

- twigs
- bamboo stick
- strong scissors or pruning shears
- school glue
- ruler
- a pencil
- modeling clay

If you don't have any bamboo, find two strong, straight twigs instead.

You may need to ask an adult to help you cut the twigs and bamboo stick.

1

Cut the bamboo sticks so that they will make a long enough ladder for your needs. Using a ruler, mark the stick at 0.5-inch (1.3 cm) **intervals.**

2

Work out how wide you want your ladder. Cut the twigs to that length. Measure each cut against the last twig you cut, so you get them pretty even.

3

Line up your two bamboo sticks on a flat surface. If they wobble or roll at all, secure them in place with a little modeling clay. Dab a little bit of strong glue onto the top mark on each stick.

4

Take a twig section and place it on the glue. It is best to leave each "rung" to dry for a while before you stick on the next one. Keep on gluing until you have completed your ladder.

Design Tips

You can make fences this way, too. You can also make fences using the same method as the ramp on page 20.

TEPEE SHELTER

A tepee at the bottom of the garden is a fun place for your fairies to play and shelter from the weather. It's easy to make.

YOU WILL NEED:
- three bamboo sticks or twigs
- a scrap of fabric
- masking tape
- strong scissors
- some string

Cut a rectangle of scrap fabric, around 5 inches (12.7 cm) by 10 inches (25.4 cm). Put some masking tape around the edge to keep the fabric from fraying.

2

Cut three lengths of bamboo that are a little longer than the shortest edge of your fabric. Tie the bamboo loosely at the top with string. Lay the sticks on the fabric.

3

Wrap the fabric around the tepee.

4

Tie string around the top of the tepee to hold the fabric in place. Make sure you can still adjust the bamboo sticks.

5

Adjust your bamboo sticks so the tepee can stand up. Cut off any **excess** fabric from the bottom of your material. Try to only cut within the area you taped.

Push the bamboo sticks into the soil.

FAIRY CHAIR

Every good garden design needs somewhere to sit. Perhaps place this little chair under the shade of a tree on a slate patio! You can make this chair using wire and a bottle cap. Thin **floral wire** is easiest to bend and cut.

YOU WILL NEED:

- floral wire
- a metal bottle cap
- strong scissors or wire cutters
- an adult to help

1

Cut two lengths of floral wire. Ask an adult to help you. Cut one length to 8 inches (20.3 cm) and another to 6 inches (15.2 cm).

2

Bend the longer wire in half to create the point of your heart-shape seat back. Place it in front of you with the pointy end facing you.

3

Now bend the two ends of the wire toward you around your thumbs to create a heart shape.

4

Make a twist in the wire. This secures your heart shape and makes the back legs.

5

Bend your second piece of wire into the shape pictured above to make the front legs.

6

Place the chair back over the front legs. Twist the front legs once around the chair back.

Design Tips

These instructions make a chair around 2.5 inches (6.3 cm) tall. This size best suits the size of a bottle cap. If you want to make a larger or smaller scale chair, you could use a jar lid or thumbtack as the seat.

GLOSSARY

conditions The circumstances or factors affecting the way in which plants are kept, especially with regard to their well-being.

convincing Capable of causing someone to believe that something is true or real.

double-sided tape Pressure-sensitive tape that is coated with adhesive on both sides. It is designed to stick two surfaces together.

drainage Holes in a pot which allow water to drain away.

excess An amount beyond what is usual, needed, or asked.

floral wire Thin wire often used in flower arrangements.

focal point The center of interest or activity.

intervals The spaces between things.

inventive Gifted with the skill and imagination to invent.

magical Having the power to control natural forces. It is possessed by certain persons such as wizards and fairies in folktales and fiction.

pea gravel Gravel consisting of small stones similar in size to peas.

pruning shears A type of scissors for use on plants.

realistic True to life or nature.

scale Size in comparison.

varnish A liquid that when spread and allowed to dry on a surface forms a hard, shiny, typically transparent coating.

FOR MORE INFORMATION

Books

Amstutz, Lisa J. *Enchanted Gardening: Growing Miniature Gardens, Fairy Gardens, and More (Gardening Guides).* North Mankato, MN: Capstone Press, 2016.

Schramer, Debbie & Schramer, Mike. *Fairy House: How to Make Amazing Fairy Furniture, Miniatures, and More from Natural Materials.* Sanger, CA: Familius, 2015.

Websites

Flea Market Gardening website with great ideas to get you started making your fairy garden
http://www.fleamarketgardening.org/2014/11/04/easy-fairy-gardens-anyone-can-do/

Publisher's note to educators and parents:

Our editors have carefully reviewed these websites to ensure that they are suitable for students. Many websites change frequently, however, and we cannot guarantee that a site's future contents will continue to meet our high standards of quality and educational value. Be advised that students should be closely supervised whenever they access the Internet.

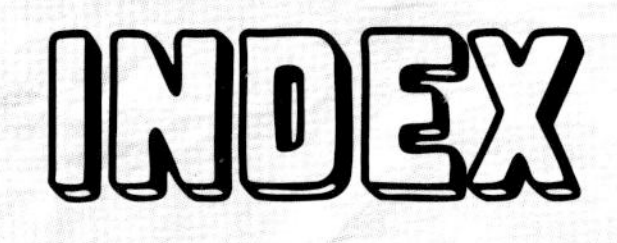

INDEX

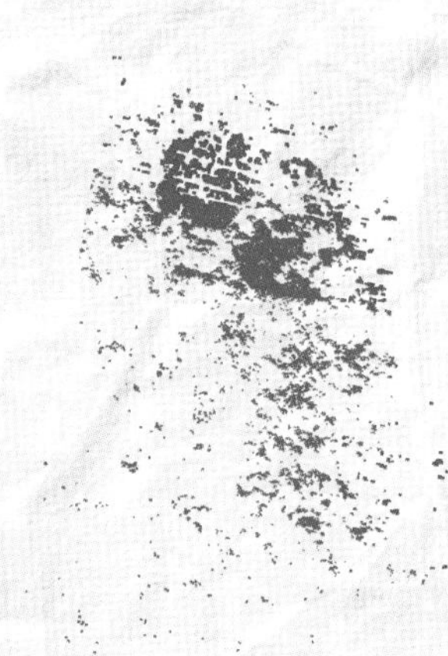